HOPE & HELP FOR MEN AS
HUSBANDS & FATHERS

MARK SHAW

INTRODUCTION

Sometimes when problems in life overwhelm us, we attempt various self-help options before we realize that we should have gone to God, our Father and Creator for the hope and help we need. It is my prayer that the booklet you are holding in your hand will give you real HOPE and practical HELP to transform your thinking and enable you to overcome the problems you are facing.

The Apostle Paul wrote, **"For whatever was written in earlier times was written for our instruction, that through perseverance and the encouragement of Scriptures,** *we might have hope"* (Romans 15:4, italics mine). Paul continued with the source of that hope: **"Now may the God of hope fill you with all joy and peace in believing, that you may abound in hope by the power of the Holy Spirit"** (Romans 15:13). Knowing God in an intimate relationship with Him as He has revealed Himself in His Word of truth and in Jesus Christ is where hope and help are truly discovered.

We should immediately turn to God's Word when we are facing various kinds of problems. All the booklets in the Hope and Help series will point you to Scripture to help you develop biblical skills and knowledge to handle problems God's way.

If you are seeking help, we would be blessed to be a resource for finding a biblical counselor in your area. You may contact us at www.histruthinlove.org or go to www.nanc.org to find a NANC certified counselor near you.

Mark E. Shaw, D.Min.
Founder and President
Truth in Love Ministries

HOPE & HELP FOR MEN AS
HUSBANDS & FATHERS

"Great job today, son! You hit two home runs and struck out six batters! You guys are going to win it all," says the proud Dad to his young son. The drive home in the car is filled with talk about the game and the future implications for the playoffs. When they get home, Dad tells his son to "hit the shower" and Dad goes to the television to relax. The son comes in and watches a show with his dad for an hour. Then Dad says, "Time for bed. Go rest that arm of yours because you may have to pitch next week." The son goes to bed and Dad and Mom spend a few minutes talking about their boy before going to sleep themselves.

The next day is Tuesday and Dad has to work late and doesn't get home until 9:30 pm. His son is already in bed. On Wednesday, Dad comes home and the family is able to eat a quick supper together, but then Dad goes outside to work on a project in his shed. He needs to do some home maintenance and spends all night working alone. When Dad gets home on Thursday, his family has gone to baseball practice followed by grocery shopping. He eats a sandwich; then gets on the internet for awhile. When his wife and son arrive home, there is little free time because the son must do his homework, shower, and go to bed. Friday is much the same in that the family members are home together in the evening, but each person does his or her own thing.

The weekend comes and Dad mows the lawn and finishes his outside work. That Saturday afternoon when the work is completed, Dad, Mom, and Son go to a movie together and grab a bite to eat. They spend a little time talking about the movie, but not much because it is late. On Sunday, they go to church together, but after that, the son goes to a friend's house for awhile, then comes home and plays outside. At bedtime there is little interaction with Dad who is busy watching football, reading, and napping. Mom is catching up on laundry and the like. A similar weekly routine like this continues for the next ten years until the son goes off to college. Unfortunately, little time is ever spent talking and listening.

What do you think of this weekly routine? How much and what kind of influence do you think Dad has had on his now adult son? How close do you think the two of them really are? How much time have they spent talking to each other? How close is Mom to Dad? Does the son feel closer to his peers and to his Mom than he does to his father? Do they really know each other? They live together, but they certainly do not know each other with much depth and intimacy.

To some degree, do you recognize this pattern in your own life? Are you the primary influence in your family's life? Is God pleased with your family relationships? Do you want to improve your relationships with your family? How can you improve them?

Modeling

Whether you realize it or not, the positive impact of a good father upon his children is tremendous. If you have a good father, can you remember how you wanted his attention and how you wanted to please him when you were a young child? "Daddy, Daddy, look at me. Watch me do this." You can often hear these statements at any playground in America. Children want to please their parents, but they particularly desire to please their *fathers* more than anyone else. (Interestingly, adult children often desire to gain a parent's approval, too, and if the desire is excessive, the adult child, as a result, may get involved with all sorts of sinful attitudes and behaviors.)

Ken Griffey, Jr. is arguably a better baseball player than his father, Ken Griffey, Sr., who was a fine baseball player at the Major League level. As a child, the younger Griffey followed his dad everywhere he could, and whenever he played with his friends he would emulate his favorite player: his father. Have you ever noticed how many athletes follow in their parents' footsteps and become athletes themselves? There are many other examples of children achieving greater success than their parents through emulation.

Modeling is an essential part of any person's development: male or female. Just look at how Jesus modeled His life before His disciples. The disciples lived with Jesus, slept where He slept, ate what He ate, watched how He ministered to hurting people, heard what He said to people, listened to Him teach the multitudes, and listened to Him instruct them privately. They did not just go hear Jesus preach a sermon once or twice a week. They gave up their previous lives to follow Him. After the resurrection of Jesus, they became significant ministers of the Gospel because they had been equipped by the Holy Spirit working in conjunction with God's Word that was "made flesh" in the Person of Jesus Christ (John 1:14).

Have you ever thought about the importance of modeling in your own life? Think about the persons who have influenced you the most and how you emulate them now. Have you picked up phrases they say? Do you have some of the same mannerisms, gestures, and body language they do? Do you think as they do on certain subjects? No matter how much you think you are an independent thinker, you are influenced by other people. 1 Corinthians 15:33 states: **Do not be deceived: "Bad company ruins good morals."** This verse is a warning that can be restated: 'Do not be prideful by thinking that you can influence a company of persons with bad morals more than they will influence you.'

Most often, bad influences will ruin your good moral thinking; therefore, you must choose wisely persons with whom you associate. Young children do not have a choice since they are born into a certain family. Children will model their parents and learn positive things like effective communication skills, resolving conflicts biblically, and setting biblical priorities. However, they can learn negative things, too, like poor ways of processing life's issues, causing angry behaviors, addictive behaviors, anxious thinking patterns, and the like. Children will learn from their parents and peers both good and bad behaviors, and quickly develop these behaviors into habits.

A man is called by God Himself into the role of being a husband and a father when the Lord blesses him with a wife and/or children. A man's role in his home as the primary influencer, teacher, counselor, instructor, discipler, and mentor is eroding in today's culture. A tremendous blessing for successful Christian living is having a godly father as an example to model. Godly fathers are becoming as extinct as the dinosaurs. What an honor it is to be a *father* because you have the privilege of being in a role that is similar to that of God the *Father's* role. You are not a perfect father as God the Father is, but you can function in a role that gives a picture of God to a young child. You are an ambassador of Christ in that you represent God to your children and Christ to your wife! (2 Corinthians 5:20, and Ephesians 6:20). It is an extremely powerful and influential position, and God has already placed you there if you have children.

A famous athlete once said that professional athletes are *not* role models. His intent may have been to get parents to see that *they* (not him) should be the primary role models for their children, which is true. However, in today's world, there is an obvious lack of biblical male and female role models for young children in their own homes, so children look outside the home. Professional athletes, music artists, movie stars, television celebrities, and the like have a greater influence upon children than their own parents do primarily because the time spent *doing things* and watching television is greater than the time spent in building family relationships. Currently, there is a whole lot of *doing* and a lot less *knowing* in the family.

Intentional Discipleship

The real key for men to understand is that spending time with children is NOT the same as modeling, discipling, and teaching children unless there is *intentional* discipleship. For example, a young child is playing with a balloon until the balloon unexpectedly pops. The child cries and comes to Dad for answers and reassurance. What does Dad need to say and do for the child at that moment? Does Dad speak the truth without love and say, "Get over it. This won't be the only balloon that ever pops in your life. You better learn to deal with disappointment." Or, does dad speak and act in love without the truth by saying, "I'm so sorry about your popped balloon. Let's go right now and buy another one for you at the store." No, the right answer comes from Ephesians 4:15 and involves "speaking the truth in love." The dad could say, "I am sorry your balloon popped, but you have to be very careful with balloons because they pop easily. I know you had fun with this one, and maybe one day soon you will get another one. For now, I realize you are sad and I understand your disappointment. Life is not perfect and there will be sad times, but God will see you through those hard times." Dad can hug the child and even pray for the child at that moment. Dad can reassure the child rather than dismiss the crying as silly or foolish and considering the child to be a nuisance to the parent. Fathers can and should deal with the issue no matter how small it is. Use every opportunity to teach your children about the Lord.

All people develop their belief systems in two primary ways. The first way people learn quickly is by reading, hearing, or seeing something they already believe to be true. If the new information agrees with what they already believe, they will often assimilate the new information into their thinking rather quickly. The second way people learn has to do with the credibility of the source of the information. If the source of the new information is known, then people will often accept it by faith. For example, the distance from earth to the sun is approximately 90 million miles. No one has actually measured that distance, but most people believe it to be true because they trust the scientists who have studied the matter. Most of *what* we believe stems from our faith in *who* we believe: scientists, friends, family, co-workers, and God.

Think about the implications of this in your family. A child who has a loving father on earth who willingly teaches his son about God the Father, is likely to believe that God the Father is good because he believes the source: his own father on earth. Of course, the Bible is the ultimate source that reveals the loving character of God, but a Christian father is a tremendous source of faith in God to a child. Ask yourself: are you increasing your family's faith in God? Are you a credible source of information in that you are living your life as obediently (not perfectly) as you can before your wife and children?

There are a number of men who profess to be Christians but their modeling (or fruit) makes that profession shaky. Are you a Christian? If not, then you must repent and believe in Christ Jesus alone to save you from your sins. If you are a Christian, then are you committed to living your life according to God's standards rather than your own? How closely are you walking with Christ now? The impact of your decision to closely follow Christ's example (model) will reverberate in the outworking of your relationships with co-workers, friends, family, and God. However, do not be deceived: your choice to obey God today will greatly affect your children, grandchildren, and great-grandchildren.

Sadly, we are discovering that many adults who are struggling with devastating problems had very little positive contact with their parents. In their childhood, the father-child relationship was non-existent, or consisted of Dad's attendance at ball games and graduation. Many counselees divulge that they love their fathers but the relationship is distant at best. Obviously, no parent is perfect and no child is permitted to respond in a sinful manner to a parent's imperfections or sin (Romans 12:17, 12:21), but the fact remains that an absentee father negatively impacts a child's development and adult life.

Absentee men come in many forms. There is the husband and father who leaves the home after a failed marriage. There is the husband and father who lives in the home but is more interested in the newspaper, internet, television, hobbies, and house projects than he is in spending time communicating with his wife and children. That father is the one depicted at the beginning of this booklet. If you are a man reading this booklet and you realize that you are in need of change because you have not been a positive influence, ambassador of Christ, and intentional role model to your wife and children, there is hope and help for you in the following pages. It may not be too late to change because children both young and old greatly desire to have a close relationship with their earthly fathers. Likewise, wives greatly desire for their husbands to love them, listen to them, and look into their eyes when communicating. Some difficult obstacles to overcome in your efforts to re-establish broken relationships may be unforgiveness, estrangement, and substance abuse, but you should make every effort to do what is right in God's eyes. In this booklet, we will give you hope and practical help in a biblically-derived model designed to restore your family relationships.

Change of Mind

Obviously, the first step is that you must have a change of mind about your role as a husband and a father. Do not believe the lies of this world and the lies of Satan that life is all about you and your goals. Your first goal must be to align your mind with the truths of God's Word. You must **"seek first the kingdom of God and his righteousness, and all these things will be added to you**. (Matthew 6:33). You must begin to search the Scriptures for God's counsel for living your life for His glory and for fulfilling the responsibilities that He has given to you in your family relationships. 1 Corinthians 10:31 states: **"So, whether you eat or drink, or whatever you do, do all to the glory of God,"** and this must begin to happen in your heart and mind first.

The Bible often calls us to repentance. "Repent" means "to turn from sin and dedicate yourself to the amendment of your life." Men do not like that word because it means realizing that you are doing something wrong or that you are failing in some way. Men don't like to ask for directions when they become lost on a family vacation, much less admit they are wrong and need God to change their minds! Nonetheless, repentance is what is required by God and it involves two things: confession of your sin and then forsaking it (or not doing it and doing the *opposite* of your sinful actions). Proverbs 28:13 states: **"Whoever conceals his transgressions will not prosper, but he who confesses and forsakes them will obtain mercy."** You need God's mercy in order to change and become the husband and father God wants you to be. That change begins with a humble heart as you admit your sin before God and your neighbors and commit to change through God's power and for His glory.

Forgiveness of Sin

Don't let pride make you hesitant to name your failures and shortcomings as "sin". Jesus died on the cross to pay the penalty required by God's justice for your sins. 1 John 1:8-9 states: **"If we say we have no sin, we deceive ourselves, and the truth is not in us. If we confess our sins, he is faithful and just to forgive us our sins and to cleanse us from all unrighteousness."** Understanding that Jesus gave His life to pay the penalty of sin is one key aspect in understanding the Gospel message. Men often do not consider it a sin to fail to spend time with their wife and children, but it is sin. There are two types of sins: commission and omission. Sins of commission are obvious because these sins are exemplified by actions such as committing murder, adultery, lying, stealing, and drunkenness. These acts of sin can be observed – they are visible actions.

Sins of omission are often more difficult to discern because nothing is visibly happening. These sins are the neglect of one's God-given responsibilities. In other words, men are failing to do something that is commanded by God. For example, God requires men to **"love your wives, as Christ loved the church and gave himself up for her"** (Ephesians 5:25). Let's say a husband comes home from work, reads the newspaper, eats dinner, gets on the internet for an hour, watches television for awhile, and reads a book until he gets tired. He goes to bed having spent little or no significant time positively interacting with his wife and children. According to the *command* of God given to this man in Ephesians 5:25 as stated above, the husband in this specific case is failing to love his wife as Christ loved the church because he is not communicating with her. Obviously, these enjoyable activities are not sinful in and of themselves. It is not what the husband is doing that is sin. It is what he is NOT doing: failing to love his wife by communicating with her. This is the standard that God requires in a marriage.

Don't be afraid to confess your sin to God because He knows it anyway. Humble yourself and confess it to Him in prayer, ask for His forgiveness, and ask Him to help you by changing your mind and heart attitudes on this issue. Then you must repent by putting forth new and opposite actions that demonstrate a total change in direction. Pray with your wife, confess your sin to her, and ask for her forgiveness. Then ask her how you can begin to demonstrate, in a practical way, your true love to her that you may keep the marriage growing in Christ. You will need the help of the Holy Spirit and God's Word as resources to enable you to change, but if you are truly willing to change, it will happen. (Only a Christian has these resources—the help of the Holy Spirit and God's Word— available to him). James 1:22-25 teaches the importance and blessing of obedient actions performed unto the Lord: **"But be doers of the word, and not hearers only, deceiving yourselves. For if anyone is a hearer of the word and not a doer, he is like a man who looks intently at his natural face in a mirror. For he looks at himself and goes away and at once forgets what he was like. But the one who looks into the perfect law, the law of liberty, and perseveres, being no hearer who forgets but a doer who acts, he will be blessed in his doing."** The goal is to please God first and to become more like Christ in your thinking, speaking, and actions. Again, you will never perfectly achieve full and complete Christ-likeness until the next life, yet God has commanded us to grow in this self-less love.

A Model for You to Follow

The apostle Paul told the Corinthians: "**Be imitators of me, as I am of Christ**" (1 Corinthians 11:1). A man must not be content to lecture and preach to his family, but he must live out his Christian life before them. Men must follow Christ's example as given in the Holy Scriptures because God wants to transform them from their old, sinful nature and conform them into the image of Christ (Romans 8:29, Romans 12:2). A man who is gradually becoming more like Jesus Christ in his thinking, speaking, and acting is a man who will experience the blessings of "**love, joy, peace, patience, kindness, goodness, faithfulness, gentleness, and self-control**" (Galatians 5:22-23) in his own life as well as in his home.*

The Word of God has been given to us to reveal God's character and to teach us how to be Christ-like. The following portion of this booklet is a biblically-derived model for men to follow and to implement in their own homes so that they can grow in their relationship with God and be more like Jesus Christ.

The Prophet, Priest, and King (Servant Leader)

Christ Jesus fulfilled three offices when He came to earth as the promised Messiah. Those offices are that of a prophet, a priest, and a king. We are given numerous pictures (or types) of these offices in the Old Testament through what we know about Elijah, Melchizedek, and David, but no man other than Jesus has or will perfectly fulfill all three of these offices. Men can learn to better function as the spiritual leaders of their homes by modeling Christ in all three of these offices, and can function as the prophet, priest, and king (servant leader) of their families.

There is a certain amount of spiritual authority in these offices but Christ fulfilled them as a *servant* not as a tyrant! Jesus gave His life in service to Christians according to Matthew 20:28: "**even as the Son of Man came not to be served but to serve, and to give his life as a ransom for many.**" Men,

10

have you given your life for your wife and children? Are you investing your life in your family relationships? Are you serving your family as the prophet, priest, and king (servant leader) of your home? As you read further, the practical ways for a man to serve his family by modeling these three offices will become clear.

* I encourage you to obtain Pastor Harry Reeder's sermon series on the Fruit of the Spirit preached at Briarwood Presbyterian Church in 2005. www.briarwood.org

Serving as "Prophet" of the Home

In the Old Testament, a prophet served God by teaching the people the will of God. He told the people what God said. Jesus was the Word made flesh (John 1:14). He revealed the character of God to the world. In the role of a prophet, Jesus authoritatively taught God's people the truth of God. In John 14:6: **Jesus said to him, "I am the way, and the truth, and the life. No one comes to the Father except through me."** Obviously, a man who is attempting to function as the "prophet" in his home is not capable of doing what Jesus did in the act of salvation for his loved ones, but a man can begin to teach his loved ones about Jesus to lead them to a saving knowledge of Christ.

How does a man function as the "prophet" of his home? A man must know the Word of God himself, and then take opportunities to teach his wife and children. He must teach them what he knows about the Word of God as he continues to learn more from a Bible-teaching church. He must begin applying God's Word to his heart and to his own life. James 1:22 states: **"But be doers of the word, and not hearers only, deceiving yourselves."** If necessary, he should find a man who can mentor him and teach him the things of God.

Sometimes a man has to remind his wife and children that God allows suffering and trials in life so that His people can become more Christ-like in character and learn to totally depend upon God alone. God's Word does not teach that

11

"God wants you to be happy at all times." Unfortunately, some parents believe this lie of the world and teach it to their children, who then have little understanding of the purpose for problems in their lives. James 1:2-4 opposes this lie by stating: **"Count it all joy, my brothers, when you meet trials of various kinds, for you know that the testing of your faith produces steadfastness. And let steadfastness have its full effect, that you may be perfect and complete, lacking in nothing."** Nowhere in these verses does God promise that you will not cry during the trial, or that you will not experience any hardship, ill will from others, hurt, rejection, or feelings of sadness. The fact that the Bible calls it a "trial" tells you that it will try your patience, intellect, and faith! For this reason, men must teach their children a biblical view of suffering with a Godly purpose of becoming more like Christ: "perfect and complete, lacking in nothing."

There are many other biblical principles to teach to your wife and children. The real problem is that many men lack the biblical knowledge, understanding, willingness, and love to teach their families God's principles for godly living. In order to be a "prophet" of God who brings the Word of Truth to his family, you must first know the Word for yourself. Spend time daily in God's Word and meditate upon a verse or a small passage of Scripture all day long. Use a study Bible to help you gain more insight into the meaning of a particular passage. Then, at least once weekly, have a short time of teaching in a "family devotion time" dedicated to helping your family better understand the Word of God. Some men have a really short family devotion after a meal together (breakfast, lunch, dinner, or evening snack), since everyone is together at the table.

No matter how you do it, you must teach your family the Word of God. Do not be concerned with the formality of teaching them because you are commanded to instruct them in various ways and places according to Deuteronomy 6:6-9: **"And these words that I command you today shall be on your heart. You shall teach them diligently to your children, and shall talk of them when you *sit* in your house, and when you** *walk* by the way, and when you *lie down*, and when you *rise*. You shall bind them as a sign on your hand, and they shall be as frontlets between your eyes. You shall *write them on the doorposts of your house* and on your gates (emphasis mine)." Whether you are teaching them to stop and pray in difficult circumstances, encouraging them to praise God for His many blessings, or writing Scripture verses on the refrigerator, you must remind them daily of the love and power of God in their everyday lives. God is interested in the details of their lives no matter how small those details seem to be. Men need to point their wife and children to Christ as often as they can.

Men are never to attempt to be the god of their wife and children by trying to control them. However, we are to function as ambassadors of Christ by being the "prophet" of the home who speaks the truth of God's Word in love to his family members as he hopes to lead them to a saving knowledge of Christ Jesus (justification) and a richer walk with Him (sanctification).

Serving as "Priest" of the Home

Old Testament priests served God's people by performing many important duties. They interceded on behalf of the people by offering sacrifices and prayers during formal worship ceremonies. A man can function as "priest" of his home by praying privately and corporately for his family. Privately, a man can pray for each member of his family to become a believer in Christ, and have a whole-hearted commitment to encourage that to happen.

Corporate prayer in the home is important and easily neglected. By corporate prayer, a man calls his family together for a designated time for prayer. The most common corporate prayer times are giving thanks prior to eating a meal and bedtime prayers, but families ought to have daily or at least weekly designated prayer times for the purpose of having the man of the home function as a "priest." During this prayer time, a man can ask each family member to submit prayer requests to him so that he may pray for those specific needs. Prayer requests can be individual needs of the person requesting prayer or they can be needs that others may have. If a family member is struggling with a prayer request, then encourage that member to think of someone for whom to pray. Get everyone to participate in the prayer request time. As the spiritual leader and "priest" of the home, you can then pray out loud using your written list of prayer requests from the family members.

When a man leads his family by praying out loud, he is doing two important things. First, he is practically demonstrating his devotion to Christ by taking these concerns to the only One who has the power to resolve the problem. It is a faith-builder and reminds everyone of their total dependence upon God the Father. Second, prayer time tends to unite the hearts of those who are praying together. Even though only one person is speaking aloud to God during the prayer, the others are listening to the words spoken in prayer and all can become like-minded around the issue. For example, a man prays for a cousin with health problems who needs physical healing along with the spiritual "healing" of the gift of eternal life. When the wife and children hear their "priest" of the home's prayer, they will know how to pray for that particular cousin in the future. Furthermore, think of this: if the cousin professes faith in Christ a few years later, the family will be reminded of how they prayed for that person and how God answered that particular prayer with a resounding, "Yes!"

While corporate and private prayer is important, do not forget to pray with each individual member when possible. Often, these one-on-one individual prayer times are spontaneous as a need arises. For example, a daughter who says, "Dad, I'm concerned about my test today in math. I studied but I know it's going to be a hard test," can be a recipient of prayer by Dad on her behalf right then. The astute dad should say, "Let's pray together right now. 'Dear Heavenly Father, we acknowledge that we are dependent upon You for all things and we ask you to be with Rebecca during her math test so that she may do her best. Lord, we ask that You would replace her fear with faith that she has prepared to the best of her ability to take this exam. Help her to do her best knowing that the results belong to You, and when it is over, I pray that she will know You in a deeper way. Amen.'"

Also, when you pray, do not be afraid to fully reveal your heart to God and to your family. If you are full of unbelief, ask God to help your unbelief (Mark 9:24). If you are fearful, ask God to "cast out" your fear with His "perfect love" (1 John 4:18). If you have been sinfully angry with your family, then during your prayer you should confess your sin to God and ask Him to help you to communicate appropriately when angry. Both God and your family members know your flaws anyway so go ahead and confess them to Him during prayer and ask Him to help you to forsake your sins. 1 John 1:9 states**: "If we confess our sins, he is faithful and just to forgive us our sins and to cleanse us from all unrighteousness."** Again, you want to model good biblical thinking and acting before your family. Model being a good "priest" before your family members, too, through the important means of prayer.

Serving as "King" (Servant Leader) of the Home

Now, the most difficult role to model is that of "king" of the home. Part of the difficulty stems from the negative connotation of a king as a tyrant and dictator. While it is true that kings were very powerful in the Old Testament, a good king served the people of God by protecting, providing for, and leading them. A servant leader is one who puts the needs of his family ahead of his own desires. An often quoted verse to husbands is Ephesians 5:25**: "Husbands, love your wives, as Christ loved the church and gave himself up for her."** A really simple and practical way to view this verse is to understand that Christ Jesus said in Luke 22:42**: "Father, if you are willing, remove this cup from me. Nevertheless, not my will, but yours, be done."** Likewise, a man can evaluate his actions by asking himself the following question: "Is this

15

action my will or God's will for my marriage and family?" A man must then evaluate his actions by comparing them to biblical principles and standards. Is he honoring God and obeying His commands or is he fulfilling a selfish desire? Is he arbitrarily making selfish decisions because he is the "king"? These are difficult questions to ask but Christ Jesus had the same challenge before Him when faced with the prospect of dying on the cross. A man can simply and practically serve his wife and children in this way: "not my will, but your will be done, God."

Jesus said in John 15:13: **"Greater love has no one than this, that someone lays down his life for his friends."** Are you laying down your life to protect your family? By protecting his family, a man provides a home that is a safe haven from the pressures and temptations of the world. A man prevents pornography from entering his home by taking safeguards against the temptation to wander the internet aimlessly. In fact, be proactive and use an internet guardian to protect all the family members. Another way that a home can be safe for a wife and children is that the husband guards himself against angry outbursts toward them. Rather than have his family feel as though they are unprotected, threatened, and attacked, a husband must strive to provide a home that is loving and peaceful. Conflicts happen but they do not have to be explosive. Conflicts can be resolved by calm communication that honors God and others.

By providing for his family, a man works hard to live within his means. Children are often more interested in having Dad's attention than in having him purchase things for them. Providing for a family is more than just providing the necessary finances; it is providing a loving environment. It is getting involved in his wife and children's lives in an intentional way. Remember that one of the names for God is "Immanuel" which means "God with us." God came down to our level. God condescended to our level in the form of Jesus Christ who walked the earth as a man. God does not expect us to understand Him at His level because we are incapable of doing so. **"For my thoughts are not your thoughts, neither** are your ways my ways, declares the Lord" (Isaiah 55:8). Do not expect your wife and children to understand your world; rather, strive to understand their world.

A man is the captain of the family ship and he sets the course of direction for everyone. A man reminds his wife and children of where they have been, how God has provided for them, and where they are headed. He must communicate clearly that he desires for his children to become believers and that their spiritual well-being is not only a temporal matter but an eternal matter. He must keep his eyes on Jesus (Matthew 14:30) and point his family to Christ for everything. He must lead them to Christ by taking them to church, praying with them, and reading God's Word to them. Look at Moses, leading people through life's wilderness is an enormous responsibility! It requires the power of the Holy Spirit and total dependence upon the grace of God.

Conclusion

A "minister" is one who serves other people. Many people think of "ministry" as feeding the hungry, providing housing for the homeless, and financially assisting the poor; however, an often neglected area of real ministry begins in the home and men are primarily responsible for being faithful for overseeing the ministry. It is the attitude of serving one's family rather than desiring to be served by them. It is intentional by looking for ways to teach and bring Christ Jesus to the remembrance of the family members. Do not aspire for approval or fame, but first look to serve your wife and children in a God-honoring manner. Matthew 20:26-28: **"But whoever would be great among you must be your servant, and whoever would be first among you must be your slave, even as the Son of Man came not to be served but to serve, and to give his life as a ransom for many."**

The responsibilities for serving one's family can be overwhelming. For this reason, one must take Proverbs 3:5-8 to heart: **"Trust in the Lord with all your heart, and do not lean on your own understanding. In all your ways**

acknowledge him, and he will make straight your paths. Be not wise in your own eyes; fear the LORD, and turn away from evil. It will be healing to your flesh and refreshment to your bones." You must begin to have the mind of Christ who said, "not my will but Your will be done," so that you can serve your family in a manner pleasing to God.

Do not neglect to read, study, memorize, and meditate upon God's Word so that you will learn the biblical principles and practical help offered in the Bible. God's Word will transform and renew your mind (Romans 12:2) and your family will reap the blessings. When you serve the Lord and seek to please Him first, not only will you reap blessings, but you will glorify the Lord through your obedience which must be your ultimate goal. Seek to glorify God in every area of your life, and send a Gospel message to each member of your family who desperately needs to better understand God's love, grace, mercy, justice, and forgiveness. Model the love of Christ before them as "prophet, priest, and king (servant leader)" of your home.

Hope & Help for Men as Husbands & Fathers

Hope & Help for Men as Husbands & Fathers